Never Chase a Man

The Secrets to Attracting And Keeping a Man
Who Values You, Loves You, And Cherishes You

MATTHEW COAST

Table of Contents

The Illusion of The Catch

"Never love anyone who treats you like you're ordinary."

- Oscar Wilde

Lisa is a 42 year old, successful, independent woman who has been at the top of her game.

She's an executive at a Fortune 500 company, a woman of substance and poise.

One evening at a charity gala, Lisa's eyes meet those of Michael, a charismatic and seemingly self-assured man.

The chemistry is instantaneous. Lisa has met and dated a lot of men over the years, very few who actually make her feel more anything.

Driven by her habitual goal-oriented habits that make her successful at work, Lisa decides she wants Michael to be part of her life.

She begins to invest her time, rearranging her demanding schedule to make room for him, and putting in the effort to show that she's interested.

Michael seems to be everything she's been looking for: ambitious, charming, and handsome.

But soon, Lisa finds herself entangled in the draining game of 'chase.'

Michael becomes elusive—his texts less frequent, his availability scarce. The harder Lisa chases, the further he withdraws, until one day, he's simply gone—vanished into thin air.

Lisa is left wondering:

Why did this happen?

She had so much to offer. She was willing to invest in a quality relationship, both emotionally and financially.

Yet, she found herself running in circles, chasing a mirage that looked like the perfect relationship.

Sound familiar?

Welcome to "Never Chase a Man," the book that aims to turn the tables.

In these chapters, you'll learn why the 'chase' is an illusion, how to recognize your own worth, and why you should never compromise your standards in the pursuit of commitment.

This book is not about game-playing, but about understanding the psychological and emotional dynamics that underlie dating and relationships.

You'll discover how to approach dating with the same level of sophistication, empowerment, and nuance that you apply in other areas of your life.

Even if he's pulling away or going cold, even if you think he's the perfect man, even if you think it's in your nature to go after what you want in life, DO NOT CHASE HIM.

If you're chasing him, he's going the wrong way. If you're chasing him, you're likely to just chase him right out of your life.

Read on to learn how to stop chasing him, and instead get him to:

- Feel closer to you

- Value you

- Fall in love with you

- Start *chasing after you.*

"Thanks to all your training my life has completely turned around and I've attracted the most amazing Man and friends and Job into my life."

- Deborah

Why Am I Talking to You About This?

I'm Matthew Coast, a name that might already ring a bell if you've ever ventured into the nuanced world of dating and relationships.

Since 2005, I've been a relentless force in the industry—initially guiding men and, for the better part of my career, shifting focus to empower women in their pursuit of fulfilling, lasting relationships.

I've been privileged to advise hundreds of thousands of women across the globe, from diverse cultural backgrounds, age groups, and life situations.

Whether you're a college student in your late teens or a vivacious 80-year-old, I've been there to provide insight, strategies, and support.

My clientele is as varied as the human experience itself—politicians, Hollywood celebrities, professional athletes, business leaders, single mothers, retirees, the divorced, and many more have sought my guidance.

While the nuances may vary, the psychological underpinnings of human connections remain largely consistent. It's this core understanding that has fueled my success and, more importantly, the happiness of the women who've trusted me.

But let's dial back the years a bit.

My journey into becoming an industry standard didn't start atop a pedestal; it began in a seat much like yours—a client seat, to be exact.

Back in 2003, I entered this sphere seeking answers to my own dating dilemmas.

My personal triumphs propelled me from client to coach, as men initially sought my expertise in navigating the dating labyrinth.

Two decades and countless success stories later, I can say I've seen the landscape from every conceivable angle.

And if there were a monumental mistake that sabotages relationships, setting them up for failure, it would undoubtedly be this: the perilous trap of 'chasing' a man.

So, if you're tired of playing catch-up in a game where the rules seem forever stacked against you, you're in the right place.

With my years of expertise and a client success rate that speaks for itself, I invite you to a transformative journey—breaking free from the cycle of 'chasing' and embracing a love life that leaves you fulfilled, valued, and ecstatically happy.

"I used some of Matt's suggestions right away with a guy who seemed to ghost on me. It. Freakin.' WORKED. It goes against what I've believed in all this time (I'm 52) cuz I'm one of those, "but it's TRUTH! WE MUST BE TRUTHFUL" But that obviously wasn't working so I thought, hey, I can still be truthful without being the guy's moral police. That's on him. So I applied my new learning and I will continue to use it. And thanx Matt."

- Lisa

The Science Behind Why Chasing Him Is a Losing Game

"The most fundamental aggression to ourselves, the most fundamental harm we can do to ourselves, is to remain ignorant by not having the courage and the respect to look at ourselves honestly and gently."

- Pema Chödrön

In this pivotal chapter, we're diving deep into the psychological truths that underscore why you should never chase a man. This isn't just feel-good rhetoric; it's backed by decades of scientific research and sociological studies.

The Magnetic Pull of Secure Attachment

Remember Lisa from our opening story?

Imagine her life as a magnet—strong, reliable, and secure.

According to Attachment Theory, conceived by psychologists John Bowlby and Mary Ainsworth, being a "secure magnet" attracts equally stable and confident partners.

Secure individuals are less likely to indulge in the fruitless game of chasing, thereby attracting relationships that are more mutual, respectful, and lasting.

Key Takeaway: Your secure attachment isn't just good for you; it's magnetic for the right kind of partner.

The Subtle Power of Less Is More

Willard Waller, a pioneering sociologist, coined the Principle of Least Interest. In any relationship, the partner who is less emotionally invested holds the reins.

When you chase, you surrender that power, allowing the other person to dictate the pace and terms of the relationship.

Let's visualize it through the metaphor of dance. If you've never done partner dancing, I highly recommend it.

I was a swing dancer for a few years so I like to reference it because of the parallels.

In swing, there's a balance that needs to be made… you pull apart, you come together, it creates tension and excitement and develops the beauty of the dance.

If you're constantly stepping forward, your partner is likely to step back, making it awkward and making it feel less like a dance and more like you're trying to force something to happen that doesn't make sense.

Part of the beauty of the dance of dating is that you're learning about each other, you're not sure, you're finding out more, and then you come together in desire because you both want to be there.

Key Takeaway: By taking a step back, you're not disengaging; you're inviting him to step forward into a balanced dance of love.

The Rarity of the Diamond

Remember how you felt the last time you discovered something rare—a collector's edition book, perhaps, or a limited-edition handbag?

Your heart raced; you knew you had to have it. That's the Scarcity Principle, articulated by Robert Cialdini.

By not chasing a man, you become that rare, precious diamond he realizes he doesn't want to lose.

Key Takeaway: Scarcity elevates value. Your willingness to step back creates an aura of rarity around you, making you even more desirable.

The Allure of The Forbidden

Ah, Romeo and Juliet—a timeless narrative of the Romeo and Juliet Effect. Barriers intensified their love. When you stop the chase, you create a 'forbidden' allure, a barrier that often serves as a magnetic pull.

Key Takeaway: Sometimes, stepping back is stepping up the allure. Create an emotional barrier, and watch him leap over it.

Freedom to Choose: The Invisible Strings

Ever felt irritated when someone tried to make a choice for you? That's Reactance Theory at play. The moment you chase, you're taking away his freedom to choose, making you less appealing in the process.

Key Takeaway: Independence is attractive. Offer him the freedom to pursue you, and more often than not, he will.

the act of chasing doesn't just erode your personal well-being; it's a losing strategy based on the very foundations of human psychology.

You deserve a love story that is mutual, fulfilling, and places you at the center, not the periphery.

These aren't just words; these are scientifically-validated principles that offer you a roadmap to a love life as thriving as your career and personal endeavors.

So, turn the page, dear reader. A new chapter of your love life awaits, and this time, you're not chasing it—it's coming straight for you.

"Matt, thank you. Your advice really helped me get over and cope with the damage from my ex husband and have helped me to be a better woman for my now fiance of a year. We've been able to look past the damage from our ex's and our pasts. We're better together and as individuals, for ourselves and for each other. I hope God blesses you greatly for the blessings you've been to us."

- Rachel and Colton

Why It Feels So Right When It's Actually So Wrong

"The heart has its reasons of which reason knows nothing."

- Blaise Pascal

I f you've ever found yourself irresistibly drawn to the chase—compelled to pursue someone even when you know deep down it might not be in your best interest—know that it's not your fault.

The urge to chase often feels natural, almost instinctive, and there's a good reason for that.

You're operating on a complex interplay of psychological, cultural, and social influences, most of which have been quietly shaping your perceptions and reactions from behind the scenes.

The pull to chase doesn't happen in a vacuum; it's the result of forces both within and outside of you.

And by the end of this chapter, you'll understand why this paradoxical situation—where chasing love feels so right when it's actually so wrong—exists in the first place.

The Subconscious Mind: Your Silent Pilot

To begin our exploration, let's turn our attention inward to the subconscious mind.

The subconscious is the realm where memories, emotions, and instinctual reactions reside. It is also a treasure trove of survival instincts.

When your stomach growls, it's not just a signal of hunger; it's your ancient wiring telling you to find sustenance.

The same principle applies to the realm of romance.

Your subconscious mind perceives a potential partner as a 'scarce resource,' one that could impact your survival and happiness.

It urges you to chase, to secure this resource before someone else does. It's not that different from how our ancestors might have chased after a source of food or water.

Cultural Codes: The Subconscious Mind's Co-Pilot

As if navigating your subconscious wasn't complex enough, your mental programming also incorporates cultural codes.

Think of all the romantic comedies where the persistent protagonist finally wins the object of their desire after an exhausting chase.

Or consider the folklore and fairy tales we grow up with: the knight who wins the princess's heart through relentless pursuit.

I've also read feminist authors who have said that it's actually empowering to chase men, even though the results seem to rarely indicate this unless you're going for a man who is looking to play the back seat to you.

If you are, there's nothing wrong with that. I have friends who have gotten married where the woman is the strong, masculine figure in the relationship and the man is the more feminine, soft figure.

And it works for both of them and they love it. So no judgment here... most women who come to me though are looking for either a masculine man or something in the middle... at the very least, a caring guy who has a backbone of some sort.

I will say that being in the feminine traditional role usually benefits the woman a lot more than the man.

We'll talk more about that in the coming chapters.

For now, just know that these narratives seep into our subconscious, reinforcing the idea that chasing is not only acceptable but romantic and valiant.

Family and Peer Expectations

It's not just the media; your family and peer circles also come with their unique sets of expectations.

Whether overt or unspoken, these norms exert additional pressure to pursue relationships actively.

"When are you settling down?"

"He's such a catch; you should hold on to him!"

These well-meaning comments further fuel your subconscious urge to chase.

Societal Systems: An External Influence

Modern society itself sets up systems that encourage the chase.

Dating apps are a prime example.

They offer an illusion of abundance, making it appear as though there are endless opportunities for love.

Yet, these platforms are designed for continual swiping, for the chase, feeding into the subconscious belief that you need to chase to find someone truly special.

They also make you focus on the most superficial aspects of a man, leading you to attract the wrong kinds of men because you're focusing on the wrong traits.

But that's a conversation for a different book.

The Confusing Interplay: The Nexus of Forces

So here you are, at the intersection of ancient survival instincts, cultural narratives, and modern societal systems.

It's a confusing place to be, and no wonder you feel the way you do. These layers of influence converge to create a powerful urge to chase, even when your rational mind tells you otherwise.

The Path Forward: Conscious Choices in Love

While it's not your fault that you've felt compelled to chase, understanding these dynamics equips you with the power to make different choices moving forward.

By recognizing the forces at play, you can start to deconstruct the urge, asking yourself:

"Is this my true desire or the result of my subconscious and societal programming?"

By asking this question, you create a space between impulse and action, a space where conscious choice resides.

And in that space, you'll find the freedom to seek love in a way that aligns with your true self, not just the layers of influence that have shaped you until now.

"It works! Matthew, I am so grateful for all of the videos. The past two and a half months have been almost more than I could take, but we managed to compromise and put things back together, starting around New Years. Thank you!"

- Amanda

What Healthy Love Looks Like

"Love does not consist in gazing at each other, but in looking outward together in the same direction."

- Antoine de Saint-Exupéry

In the quest for love, the difference between chasing and being pursued is like night and day.

The previous chapter peeled away the layers behind why the chase feels so instinctive yet can be so damaging.

But what does a healthy attraction look like?

How can we identify a balanced dynamic where both partners are invested, yet the man is making that extra effort, tilting the scales toward a lasting, committed relationship?

In this chapter, we unfold a real-life story that encapsulates this ideal—where connection is not a tug-of-war but more of a harmonious dance.

Sarah was a successful consultant in a bustling city, content in her life but missing that special connection.

Alex, a charismatic engineer, met her at a mutual friend's party.

Unlike previous experiences, Sarah felt a magnetic pull but didn't feel the need to orchestrate every move.

Alex took the initiative, asking her out to an art gallery and dinner after.

Sarah was intrigued. She enjoyed art, and it wasn't the standard 'drinks at a bar' invitation. On the date, the conversation flowed naturally, punctuated by bouts of laughter and shared values. Sarah felt at ease.

She was interested but not anxious. Alex was similarly engaged, asking questions and sharing his thoughts but without the suffocating intensity she'd often felt from other men.

While Sarah reciprocated interest, she didn't find herself checking her phone obsessively or initiating every interaction.

Alex was putting in that extra effort. He planned thoughtful dates, remembered details from their conversations, and expressed his feelings at a pace that felt comfortable for both.

About three months into dating, Alex brought up the topic of exclusivity.

Sarah felt a surge of happiness; she'd been hoping for this but hadn't felt the need to push the subject.

Alex took the lead, and it felt organic—almost like he was reading her mind. The relationship progressed, and while they both put in effort to sustain it, Sarah could sense that Alex was fully committed to building something long-term.

What was remarkably different in Sarah and Alex's story was Alex's consistent effort.

Whether it was planning a weekend getaway, cooking dinner together, or discussing future plans, Alex was always one step ahead in making sure their relationship thrived.

Sarah and Alex's story isn't a fairy tale; it's a testament to what happens when two people engage in a balanced dynamic of pursuit and mutual interest.

Sarah never had to chase or feel like she was doing the heavy lifting.

Alex, in his genuine interest and commitment, naturally took on that role, embodying the masculine energy that complements feminine grace so beautifully.

If you'd like support and to join a group of women who are at various stages of the same path of attracting the man and having the relationship they want, check out our Facebook Group here…

https://www.facebook.com/groups/goddesscommunity

5 Reasons Why You Should Never Chase a Man

"You cannot convince people to love you. This is an absolute rule. No one will ever give you love because you want him to give it. Real love moves freely in both directions. Don't waste your time on anything else."

– Cheryl Strayed

Engaging in the dating world can often feel like a game—strategies to implement, roles to play, and hearts to win or lose.

Yet, the tendency to chase after a man, well-intended as it may be, is often counterproductive to forming a lasting, committed relationship.

Here are the five compelling reasons why chasing a man will not only not get him to invest in you but also jeopardize your chances of creating a love story that stands the test of time.

1. THE EMOTIONAL STOCK MARKET: THE EASE OF WALKING AWAY

Let's delve into the dynamics of human behavior and relationships with what I call the "Investment Principle."

This psychological axiom suggests that the more resources—be it time, energy, or emotional bandwidth—you pour into someone or something, the more value it holds for you, making you more afraid of losing it.

Investment in Everyday Life

Imagine you're an art collector, and you spend years searching for a masterpiece.

You finally find one, invest a small fortune into acquiring it, and even more effort into maintaining its pristine condition.

The emotional and financial investment in this piece of art makes it almost unbearable to think about parting with it.

Applying the Investment Principle to Relationships

In the romantic arena, if you're doing all the chasing—calling, planning dates, initiating conversations—you become like that art collector, emotionally entangled in the 'masterpiece' that is this man.

However, the twist is that he hasn't invested a single cent or an ounce of effort into acquiring you. Consequently, for him, walking away becomes as easy as returning a trinket bought on impulse.

Simultaneously, your investment roots you deeper into the relationship, making it agonizingly difficult for you to disengage.

What you ideally want is a situation where he feels as though he has found his irreplaceable masterpiece in you, leading him to invest effort, energy, and emotion.

Only then will he find it challenging to walk away, developing a profound sense of attachment and commitment.

2. THE PRECEDENT OF LAZINESS: WHEN EFFORT BECOMES OPTIONAL

Once you put in all the initial effort, you inadvertently set the tone for the entire relationship—a tone that can be incredibly hard to change later on.

You essentially communicate that you will be the one steering the ship, while he merely has to sit back and enjoy the ride.

The Vicious Cycle of Overcommitment

Picture yourself organizing a dinner party. You handle the invitations, buy the groceries, prepare the meal, and even clean up afterward.

What happens at the next gathering? People expect you to shoulder the burden again.

Why?

Because you've set a precedent, and they see no reason to step up.

In the same way, your relationship can become a one-sided dinner party where you're doing all the cooking and cleaning.

While this arrangement might seem acceptable at first, over time it leads to a toxic imbalance.

Breaking the Cycle

Rather than setting a precedent where you are doing all the work, aim for a relationship where both parties are active contributors.

And if commitment has not yet been established, ensure that he's investing more time, effort, and emotion into the relationship than you are.

Otherwise, you risk entering into a vicious cycle where he becomes comfortable doing less and less as you do more and more.

3. THE PSYCHOLOGY OF GRATITUDE: WHY BEING TAKEN FOR GRANTED IS ALMOST GUARANTEED

You may think that if you're pulling all the weight, he would appreciate you more. Surprisingly, the opposite tends to be true.

According to psychology, people place greater value on the things they have to work for.

The Paradox of Free Lunch

Think about the saying, "There's no such thing as a free lunch."

Even if someone offers you something at no cost, you tend to question its value.

When something is freely given, we often take it for granted, ignoring its intrinsic value and the effort someone made to provide it.

Whenever I give my friends free concert tickets, they never seem to show up… we value things that we pay for, invest in, and put energy, emotion, and effort into.

Turn the Tables: Making Him Invest

In the world of romance, this principle holds.

If you're the one investing all your time, energy, and emotional capital into the relationship, you'll inevitably value him more, simply because you've had to work for it.

Conversely, if he hasn't had to lift a finger, he won't see your worth in the same way.

That's why, to ensure a lasting, equitable relationship, you should insist that he invests in you—whether it be his time, his energy, or his emotional attention.

4. THE AMBIGUITY TRAP: WHEN HE'S UNSURE ABOUT YOUR FUTURE TOGETHER

When a man isn't putting in the effort, he won't value the relationship in the way he should. This emotional disconnect often manifests as indecision about where your relationship is headed.

The Never-Ending Loop of "I Don't Know"

Picture a student who never studies but still manages to scrape by with passing grades.

This student never fully commits to academic success and, as a result, never truly understands the material.

Similarly, if he's not invested, he won't see the relationship as something serious, creating a never-ending loop of uncertainty.

He will avoid conversations about commitment, leaving you in limbo and feeling emotionally adrift.

The Ripple Effect on Your Self-Worth

This uncertainty isn't just damaging to your relationship; it can also wreak havoc on your self-esteem.

Many women find themselves questioning their value when faced with a man who won't commit or seems perpetually confused about what he wants.

You deserve better.

The Clarity You Deserve

Remember, a man who truly values you won't be wishy-washy about your future together.

He'll be eager to make plans, to build something meaningful.

The more he values you, the more he'll want to talk about and invest in a future together—giving you the clarity and commitment you deserve.

5. THE INVESTMENT EQUATION: WHY HE WON'T FALL AND STAY IN LOVE IF YOU'RE CHASING

Perhaps the most telling reason why chasing is counterproductive comes down to a simple formula:

His level of investment in you directly correlates with the depth of his emotional attachment.

The Mental Gymnastics of Investment

Imagine you've spent months building a complex sandcastle.

Each day, you painstakingly add more turrets, carve intricate designs, and fortify the walls. Would you let a high tide come and wash it away without a second thought?

Absolutely not.

You'd protect it because you've invested so much into it.

Similarly, when a man invests in you, he goes through a sort of emotional reasoning. He starts to ask himself why he's putting in all this effort.

And the conclusion he'll arrive at is simple: he must be doing it because he's falling for you.

The Seeds of Lasting Love

The key to a man's heart—and to keeping him deeply in love—is getting him to invest in you emotionally.

By creating an environment where he's contributing his time, energy, and emotional currency, you're planting the seeds for a love that can stand the test of time.

Your relationships should never be built on the shaky ground of one-sided investment.

Keep the scales balanced—or better yet, tipped in your favor—and you'll cultivate a love that's not only passionate but also steadfast and enduring.

"This program works! I found a boyfriend, we dated, he proposed to me today! I'm so happy!"

- Emily

The Chase Detective: 7 Signs You're Doing The Chasing

"Never make someone a priority when all you are to them is an option."

- Maya Angelou

Awareness is the first step to change.

It's crucial to recognize the signs that you're unintentionally chasing him.

This can be a tricky area to navigate because it's all too easy to rationalize our actions in the name of love or connection.

Let's delve into these indicators that show you might be in pursuit rather than being pursued.

1. THE ONE-SIDED CONVERSATION STARTER

The first tell-tale sign is straightforward: Are you the one always reaching out? Whether it's texting, calling, or even Morse code, if you find that you're initiating more than half of the conversations, it's time to reassess.

Entering the 'over 50% zone' creates a risky dynamic, one where the scales of investment tip unfavorably in his direction.

The Ideal Communication Ratio

Though some advice might tell you never to initiate, the truth lies in a more balanced approach.

Aim for a range where you're initiating between 20% and 50% of the time. Cross over the 50% threshold, and you risk losing his interest; go under 20%, and he might think you've lost interest.

2. THE CONVERSATION LIFELINE

If you find yourself struggling to keep conversations alive, as if you're trying to resuscitate a dying fire, it's another sign you're chasing.

Maybe you're talking about the weather or the latest Netflix show just to fill the silence.

Tips to Turn the Tide

Embrace the Silence: It's okay to have moments of quiet. Take this time to feel connected to the present moment, grounding yourself in your own thoughts and feelings.

Affirm Your Worth:

Practice affirmations like, "I am worthy of being pursued," or "I am a beautiful, captivating woman."

These are not just words; they're beliefs that can change your behavior and energy.

For a deeper dive into affirmations, refer to my Forever Woman program.

Be Present in Your Body: Instead of mentally scrambling for the next topic, take a few deep breaths and reconnect with your sensations and emotions.

Self-Connection: Finally, spend quality time with yourself. Often when we're overly focused on someone else, it's because we've lost our center.

Reconnect with your hobbies, your friends, and what makes you unique.

By recognizing and addressing these signs, you can reset the balance, making room for him to step up and chase you instead.

Remember, it's not about playing hard to get; it's about setting the stage for a more balanced, reciprocal, and fulfilling relationship.

3. THE UNOFFICIAL DATE PLANNER

One unmistakable sign you're doing all the chasing is if you find yourself acting as the unofficial planner for every outing, every date, and every rendezvous.

If you're at the point where nothing happens unless you organize it, consider this a red flag.

Utilize the Scarcity Principle

Remember the Scarcity Principle?

People value what is scarce.

If he's not putting in the effort to plan and spend quality time with you, make it a requirement.

Your time, presence, and effort are valuable commodities.

Make him earn the privilege of spending time with you.

The Intimacy Clause

As for physical intimacy, it's a hot-button topic.

If you're comfortable sharing that level of closeness without requiring any emotional investment, that's your prerogative.

However, psychology suggests that people, including men, tend to value what they've worked hard to attain.

If a committed, valued relationship is your goal, requiring effort on his part before progressing to physical intimacy can set that standard.

4. THE ASYMMETRY OF TIMELINESS

Have you ever noticed how quickly you respond to his messages compared to his response time to yours?

Does your phone barely finish buzzing before you've fired off a reply, while his replies might take hours or even days?

This lopsided dynamic is another indicator you're doing the chasing.

How to Rebalance the Scales

Engagement Gauge: If he's not active in the conversation, it's not worth diverting your attention to keep it going. You should both be contributing to the dialogue.

Don't Pause Life: Don't halt what you're doing just to respond to him. Continue with your activities; you are a person with a life and priorities. Show him that your time is valuable.

Master of Cliffhangers: Ending conversations on a note of mystery or promise can do wonders.

For example, if he asks about weekend plans, you might reply, "I have something interesting lined up.

Can't wait to share it with you." This sets up an expectation and makes room for him to step into the role of the chaser.

By recognizing these signs and implementing these tips, you're not only preserving your dignity but also making room for a more balanced, respectful, and fulfilling relationship.

Let him put in the work to earn your time and affection; it will only make the relationship more valuable in his eyes, and yours.

5. ONE-SIDED TRANSPARENCY

If you find yourself constantly opening up, sharing your deepest feelings and experiences, while he remains an enigma, this is a clear sign you're doing the chasing.

Emotional investment should be reciprocal in a relationship that's progressing toward something meaningful.

Ways to Open Him Up:

Ask Open-Ended Questions: These types of questions can't be answered with a simple 'yes' or 'no,' and they invite him to share more.

Delve Deeper: If he gives you a surface-level answer, ask follow-up questions to encourage him to dig deeper into his thoughts and feelings.

Patient Listening: Resist the urge to fill awkward silences or complete his sentences. Give him space to express himself.

Find His Passion Point: Almost everyone has a topic they can talk about for hours. Find his and let him open up.

6. EMOTIONAL BURNOUT

It's draining, isn't it?

Being the one who's always planning, texting, caring, and sharing can lead to emotional exhaustion.

It's an unfortunate reality that many women face. But know this—you're not alone, and you deserve better.

The Mirror Technique:

Reflect His Level of Investment: Pay close attention to how much effort he's putting into the relationship.

Are his actions reciprocating your level of commitment? Mirror this level of investment positively.

You Deserve Reciprocity: A balanced relationship requires two people who are both willing to put in effort.

Your emotional, mental, and physical investments should be valued and reciprocated.

Your Worth: Always remember your value.

You are someone worth investing time, energy, and emotion in. Don't let anyone make you feel otherwise.

Set Boundaries: If he's not willing to invest in you, it might be time to reconsider the relationship. Relationships are not one-sided; they require effort from both parties.

The bottom line is this: If you're the only one investing your time, emotions, and energy into the relationship, it's not a sustainable or satisfying situation.

Turn the tables by understanding your worth and demanding the love and respect you unquestionably deserve.

Take steps to redress the balance and allow room for a more equitable, fulfilling relationship.

7. THE PERILS OF PUSHING FOR PROGRESS

If you find yourself doing all the heavy lifting when it comes to pushing the relationship forward, that's a glaring red flag.

The path to a committed, loving relationship should not be a solo trek. When it's the right fit, both parties will be actively engaged in deepening the bond.

The Pitfall of Unreciprocated Efforts:

1. Commitment Isn't One-Sided: You shouldn't be the only one striving to elevate the relationship to the next level. It's a collective endeavor.

2. Don't Swim Alone: Before you dive into the deep end of commitment, make sure he's willing to jump in with you. Otherwise, you risk finding yourself swimming in circles, alone.

3. Beware of Passive Players: Some men might seem content letting you take the reins because it satisfies their needs with minimal effort on their part.

This is a dangerous dynamic that devalues your worth in the relationship.

How to Shift the Dynamics:

1. **Identify the Imbalance**: Acknowledge that you're doing all the pushing. The first step to solving a problem is recognizing that there is one.

2. **Set Clear Expectations**: Have an open dialogue where you both can express your relationship goals. If he's hesitant or evasive, it's a telling sign.

3. **Pull Back**: Withdraw some of your emotional and logistical investment and observe how he reacts.

Does he step up, or does the relationship stall?

This is a crucial test of his interest and investment in you.

4. **Remember Your Worth**: Your love, time, and emotional energy are invaluable resources. Do not squander them on someone who doesn't appreciate them.

In summary, if you're the only one pushing for relationship milestones, then it's time for a gut check.

A meaningful relationship demands mutual investment.

Stick to this non-negotiable rule: do not over-invest in a man who under-invests in you.

Doing so safeguards your emotional well-being and paves the way for a more balanced, fulfilling relationship.

"I should say Thank you Matthew. I had totally lost self-confidence. I was almost forgetting my worth after going through an abusive relationship but finding you brought me back to life. I love you Matthew, may God continue blessing and using you."

- Rachel

The Alternative Path to Chasing

You cannot save people, you can only love them."

- Anais Nin

Based on years of experience and interactions with countless women, it's clear: women don't just want to be another face in the crowd. They want to be the unforgettable person that a man values and desires for a lifetime.

That's why I've developed a five-step strategy, designed to offer you a powerful alternative to the wearisome game of chase.

By following these steps, you'll position yourself as an irreplaceable presence in his life.

STEP ONE: REORIENT YOUR AIM

If you're focusing exclusively on capturing his attention, you're actually pushing him away.

The more you aim to prove your worth to him, the less likely he will see it for himself. Instead, redirect your focus toward the bigger picture—the kind of relationship you desire.

This is something I call, **Relationship Over Man.**

If your focus is on getting the man, you'll end up putting him on a pedestal, making everything about him, and trying to manipulate your way into making him be the right man for you.

This ends in heartbreak, I promise you.

Instead, you take the man off of the pedestal and you put the relationship there.

You stop making the man the goal and you start making the relationship the goal.

You then determine whether he's going to take you to the relationship you want or not.

If he is, great. He'll take you there. If not, you'll find a better man who will.

And he's more likely to take you there if you stop focusing on him and start focusing on the relationship.

Again, this is "Relationship Over Man" and it works.

This perspective shift isn't just about semantics; it's about redefining your romantic trajectory.

The key is a mindset transformation.

STEP TWO: BE AUTHENTICALLY INTERESTED

Here's where the 'Attainability Principle' comes into play.

The principle states that people are more likely to chase what they believe they can catch.

Translate this to dating: if he doesn't think a relationship with you is within his reach, he's not going to invest.

Many women think that "leaning back"—avoiding the initiation of contact or showing any overt interest—is the secret sauce to get him pursuing them.

This is a fallacy.

Consider the psychology of video gaming: games become addictive because they offer staggered achievements and dopamine boosts.

But, if a game becomes impossible to win, even the most ardent gamer will quit.

I've seen numerous cases where women don't make it past the initial dates because men feel a relationship is unattainable, regardless of the woman's attractiveness or qualities.

The trick here is balance. A flirtatious message or a casual call to show you're thinking about him can go a long way.

Avoid the extremes—being overly available or completely aloof. Aim for the golden mean, where your interest is clear, but not overwhelming.

The Magic is in the Middle, remember that.

STEP THREE: MASTER THE ART OF BEING PURSUED

One cornerstone of my coaching philosophy is the Investment Principle. This is rooted in behavioral psychology—namely the concept known as the 'sunk cost fallacy.'

When a man invests his time, energy, and emotion in you, he begins to perceive you as a valuable asset in his life, one he's not eager to relinquish.

Think of it like planting seeds in a garden: the more he nurtures the relationship, the less willing he'll be to walk away and let the garden wither.

Flip the script, and if you're the one doing all the chasing, you become the invested party. Your attraction to him becomes amplified, regardless of his feelings toward you.

The key here isn't just love; it's about a holistic blend of respect, mutual values, and emotional connection.

Picture your emotional and logical faculties as two wings of an eagle; you need both to soar successfully in the realm of romance.

Here are some tactical ways to get him invested:

Establish your preferences subtly, using phrases like, "I really appreciate when…" or "What I find attractive is…" to set behavioral standards.

Make small requests. Ask him to hold your coat, or fetch your drink. Small investments on his part lead to bigger emotional stakes.

Aim for balanced initiation. Maintain a 2:1 or 3:1 ratio in initiating contact, so both parties feel invested in maintaining the connection.

STEP FOUR: LEAVE ROOM FOR MYSTERY

This brings us to the 'Law of Familiarity,' which posits that excessive exposure can breed contempt—or at the very least, indifference.

Picture it like a favorite song on repeat: played too often, even the most enchanting tune can lose its allure.

I remember coming home from military service; the initial excitement of my return gradually dimmed as my continued presence became the norm.

Absence, as they say, makes the heart grow fonder. Being ever-present in his life won't provide him the room to miss you or chase you.

Here, the 'Law of Identification' comes into play.

Constant togetherness can meld two individual identities into one, making breakups feel like a physical part of you has been torn away.

To prevent this, fortify your own identity. Pursue your interests, refine your hobbies, and engage in activities that bolster your sense of self.

The stronger your individual identity, the healthier your relationship will be—and the more he'll work to keep you in his life.

STEP FIVE: UNLOCK THE GATEWAY TO HIS HEART

At its core, forming an emotional bond is about tapping into the inner recesses of his heart.

While many women attempt to appeal to men through superficial traits or qualities they themselves find attractive, the real magnetism lies in who you truly are—the ineffable essence that makes you, you.

Let's delve into the 'Emotional Range Principle,' a two-fold approach to fostering a deep emotional connection:

The Internal Pathway: The first route to his heart is through your own.

By nurturing a strong emotional connection with yourself, you naturally extend this emotional bridge to him.

Think of it as a lighthouse: by illuminating your own emotional landscape, you become a beacon that draws him in.

The External Pathway: This involves sculpting emotionally-rich moments within your interactions.

You can achieve this by steering conversations toward topics that light him up—his passions, dreams, or even things that make him laugh.

When you invite him to share what excites him, a magical cascade effect occurs. He begins to associate those uplifting emotions with your presence.

Picture it as a favorite melody: whenever it plays, he'll unconsciously relate the joy it sparks to you.

In essence, these methods help create the initial threads of an emotional tapestry.

However, to weave a lasting bond, what ultimately matters is his connection with the authentic you—the person you are at your core, sans any pretenses.

"You helped me go from an abusive mind set my ex husband did to me. To a mind set that I am worth something to someone. My current boyfriend is very patient. I am not ready for marriage but you have helped me out a lot. So I say thank you."

- Phyllis

The Art of 'Leaning Back': How to Master the Dance of Attraction

"Do not bring people in your life who weigh you down. And trust your instincts ... to make the choices you need to make. You are smarter than you think. And you are stronger than you know."

- Oprah Winfrey

Earlier in our discussion, we touched upon the concept of 'leaning back,' a term that might seem nebulous to some. However, its premise is simple yet profoundly effective: by leaning back, you empower yourself, inviting him to chase and invest in you.

Let's paint this concept through the lens of a dance. Imagine you're waltzing with your partner. If you lean forward aggressively, you risk stepping on his toes or losing your own balance. In contrast, leaning back transforms you into a graceful dancer, eliciting the natural urge in him to step forward and take the lead.

'Leaning back' is more than just a dating tactic—it's a paradigm shift that reframes how you approach love and attraction. It elevates your worth in his eyes, prompting him to invest more effort in winning your heart. Moreover, it serves as a litmus test to gauge his true feelings, and places you in a position of power—empowering you to shape the relationship you desire rather than settling for less or resigning from dating altogether.

THE DO'S OF LEANING BACK

If your goal is to cultivate a fulfilling relationship where you are deeply cherished, keep reading to master the art of leaning back.

1. Craft an Inviting Space: Consider your life a beautiful mansion. You're not forcing him through the front door; you're leaving it ajar, subtly inviting him in. Imagine clearing out a room in your metaphorical mansion, making it warm and welcoming—just for him. This act of leaning back entails:

- Halt the barrage of texts and calls: Give him room to reach out first.
- Cease to chase him: Allow him to set the pace.
- Resist the urge to gift him constantly: Let him treat you as well.
- Refrain from seeking constant validation: Your worth is inherent; it's not defined by his opinion.
- Stop the 'overdoing': Remember, a partnership is a two-way street.

2. Detach from His Digital Life: Social media is often a rabbit hole that leads to anxiety and over-analysis. "Why is he active but not messaging me? Who is this other woman he's talking to?" If it takes a digital detox to refrain from stalking his online behavior, then so be it.

3. Open Communication: While the crux of leaning back is to let him take the reins, it's only fair to give him a heads up if there's a shift in dynamics. Casual yet deliberate communication can make all the difference: "Hey, I'm going to be tied up with work this week. Feel free to message me when you're free." This throws the ball in his court and grants you the space to observe his next move, thus revealing his level of interest.

Mastering the art of leaning back is akin to performing an elegant dance. It creates a gravitational pull that draws him toward you, all while enabling you to hold your ground—elegant yet empowered.

The Essentials of 'Leaning Back': The Next Steps for Mastery

Having discussed the art of 'leaning back,' let's delve deeper into the crucial steps that build on this transformative approach to dating and relationships.

As we progress, remember that each step is a piece of a larger puzzle that creates an image of a self-empowered, radiant woman who effortlessly draws love and respect into her life.

The Advanced Do's of Leaning Back

4. Refocus on Your Well-Being: Think of it as redirecting a spotlight from him to yourself. Shift your energy into activities that nourish your soul and wellbeing—whether that's diving into a new hobby, enhancing your career skills, or simply indulging in self-care. This transition isn't about excluding him; it's about creating an enriched life that he'd feel privileged to be part of.

5. Share Your Vibrant Life with Him: As you embark on these new activities, let him in on what's exciting you these days. By doing so, you achieve two key objectives: it dismisses any notion that you've lost interest in him and simultaneously deepens your emotional connection by sharing your passions. Let him know that although your calendar is filling up, you're open to spending quality time when he's available.

6. Expand Your Dating Horizon: If your relationship hasn't been defined as exclusive, allow yourself the liberty of exploring other connections. It's not about creating jealousy; it's about recognizing your worth and maintaining an open field until a commitment is established. Even if you're in a casual arrangement, keep your options open unless exclusivity has been explicitly discussed.

7. Live in Abundance: As elaborated in my Forever Woman Program, the principle of abundance isn't confined to romantic relationships. Build a web of enriching connections, be it with friends, family, or even pets. Fill your life with positive interactions that go beyond romantic entanglements. When you emanate an aura of abundance, it becomes magnetic.

8. Be Your Own Queen: There's immense power in treating yourself with the same fervor you would a loved one. Book that spa day, buy yourself that piece of jewelry you've been eyeing, or simply spend a night pampering yourself at home. Show yourself the love you deserve, and others will follow suit.

9. Introspect on Your Tendencies: Lastly, the drive to 'lean forward' often stems from deeper insecurities or past experiences.

Take time to introspect: why do you feel the compulsive need to be the one doing all the work in relationships?

Pinpoint these root causes and work on healing. Remember, self-awareness is the first step to self-empowerment.

As you take these steps, the aim is to evolve into a woman who is not just leaning back physically, but emotionally and psychologically as well.

Each of these steps is aimed to make you a 'Forever Woman'—someone who understands her worth and doesn't compromise on what truly matters in a relationship.

It aligns perfectly with your pursuit of a meaningful, invested relationship, placing you in a position of strength and desirability.

Master these advanced steps, and you won't just be practicing the art of leaning back—you'll be living it.

NAVIGATING THE PITFALLS: THE 'DON'TS' OF LEANING BACK

Understanding the concept of leaning back is one thing, but implementing it without missteps is another. While the 'Dos' set the stage for a healthy, balanced dynamic, knowing what not to do is equally critical.

Below, I've outlined common pitfalls that women may encounter when trying to lean back, and how to avoid them while maintaining a sophisticated yet approachable demeanor.

The Sophisticated Approach to Avoiding Mistakes

1. Don't Ghost Him: Ignoring him altogether will most likely backfire and could send the message that you're uninterested or playing games. The essence of leaning back isn't about cutting off contact; it's about striking a balance.

2. Avoid Communication Blackouts: Not informing him about your change in interaction style can be confusing and may create unnecessary tension. A simple heads-up about your need to focus on other areas of your life can go a long way.

3. Don't Abandon Initiating Contact: The art of leaning back is not a one-way street. You don't have to wait for him to make all the moves.

Feel free to initiate conversations or plans, but do so in a manner that complements your new approach.

4. No Delay Tactics: Waiting excessively long to reply to his texts or calls sends the wrong message. It can come off as a strategic play rather than genuine interest, which is counterproductive to building a sincere connection.

5. Don't Become a Statue: Leaning back is not about inaction; it's about calculated action. A relationship requires investment from both parties. Don't withdraw so much that you come off as disengaged or apathetic.

6. Avoid Rigid Rules: Life is unpredictable, and your approach should be flexible enough to adapt to different situations. If he texts you about an emergency or something significant, the "rules" of leaning back can and should be momentarily set aside.

7. Don't Be Unreachable: Being perpetually busy or unavailable not only contradicts the notion of a mutual relationship but also risks portraying you as unattainable. Make time for him when you can, showing that while you have a fulfilling life, you also value his role in it.

8. Avoid the Extremes: The art of leaning back does not endorse polarized behavior—either being too clingy or too detached. Instead, it calls for a nuanced approach, tailored to the specific dynamics of your relationship.

By sidestepping these common mistakes, you remain aligned with the core principles of leaning back, allowing the relationship to develop naturally, with both parties feeling valued and invested.

This isn't about games or manipulation; it's about building a solid foundation for a relationship where both partners are equally committed and intrigued.

Be the woman who understands the delicate balance of leaning back—the one who retains her mystique while remaining genuinely involved.

LEANING BACK: SETTING THE GROUND RULES

Leaning back isn't a rigid set of guidelines; rather, it's a nuanced strategy tailored to you and your relationship.

With that said, let's delve into some general ground rules that will empower you to maintain an engaging yet respectful distance. These principles honor your self-worth and encourage reciprocal effort in the relationship.

Your Comprehensive Rulebook

1. Don't Double Text: If your text messages go unanswered, resist the urge to send another. Think of your interaction as a tennis match—both players need to take turns to keep the game going.

2. Mind Your Intentions: Before initiating a conversation, question your motives. Are you reaching out to get him to behave a certain way, or are you genuinely interested in talking? If it's the latter and his energy has been coming your way, go ahead and reach out.

3. Detach from the Outcome: If you're not overly concerned about how he will respond, feel free to text, particularly if it's been a while. This is a low-stakes way to check the pulse of his interest.

4. Allow Him Room to Lead: If you're doing all the planning and initiating, you're not giving him a chance to step up. Leaning back offers him the space to show interest and take the reins every once in a while.

5. Cultivate an Abundance of Connections: Keep engaging with other aspects of your life, including meeting other men if you're not exclusive.

This enriches your life and keeps you from getting overly invested too soon.

6. Express Appreciation and Interest: If he's putting in the effort, acknowledge it. This reinforces his actions and signals that his efforts aren't in vain. Consider this your 'invitation' for him to continue.

7. Flexibility in Application: Leaning back is not a permanent state but a tool. Depending on the health and stage of your relationship, you can choose to apply it as needed.

Striking a Balanced Equation

Remember, relationships are about equilibrium. It's about finding a dynamic that suits both parties involved.

As you navigate the leaning back strategy, use these ground rules as touchstones that keep you aligned with a balanced, mutually fulfilling relationship.

Leaning back doesn't have to be a calculated strategy; it's more of a conscious choice to let things unfold naturally.

The ultimate aim is to create a space where both partners are contributing to the relationship's growth. Lean back, but lean in when it counts, striking that elegant balance that keeps the relationship not just intact but thriving.

"He has responded in the way I was hoping he would and I'm so glad he did we are in a very committed relationship now and talking a very long term commitment and it's like I opened a book to his heart and he's very open about everything now I couldn't ask for a better man than him thank you so much I'm glad I found your help."

- Nicole

5 Unexpected Qualities That Will Make Him Chase You

"Self-worth comes from one thing:
thinking that you are worthy."

- Wayne Dyer

Captivating a man's interest goes beyond the typical allure of physical beauty and basic compatibility.

There are specific qualities that make you irresistibly chase-worthy. Here are five such qualities that, while unconventional, can make a man feel like you're the only woman he ever wants to be with:

1. UNCERTAINTY: THE SPICE OF LOVE

Imagine the thrill of a closely-matched sports game. The tension, the uncertainty, it's what keeps you on the edge of your seat.

The same principle applies to dating and relationships. Uncertainty is intriguing and addictive.

How do you incorporate this into your relationship dynamic?

You give him glimpses of your affection and interest, but never fully let him in on how much you're into him.

This doesn't mean playing manipulative games. It means being genuine but reserved in your affections.

Why it works: Men love a challenge. If he's unsure of your complete devotion, he's more likely to work to win you over.

However, remember that the magic is in the middle. You don't want him so certain of your affection that he becomes complacent, nor so unsure that he thinks you're uninterested and gives up.

The right dose of uncertainty will make him eager to invest more time and emotion into building a relationship with you.

2. A STRONG IDENTITY: THE ALLURE OF INDEPENDENCE

You are not a blank canvas waiting to be painted upon. You are a vibrant masterpiece, compelling in your individuality. When you have a strong identity, you're not just participating in life — you're leading it.

Why it works: Men are attracted to women who have passions, interests, and ambitions. A woman with a strong identity has her own life, and she's not going to put it on hold for anyone.

This presents a man with a healthy challenge: to be so compelling that you would consider incorporating him into your already fulfilling life.

You become a prize he is eager to win — but only if he proves that he's worth your time.

3. BOUNDARIES: THE INVISIBLE LURE

Boundaries aren't walls; they're guidelines that make people understand the best way to interact with you.

They're your invisible aura that commands respect and consideration.

Why it works: The stereotype that men want a woman who will let them get away with anything is misleading.

Most men, especially those looking for a serious relationship, respect a woman who has clear boundaries.

It suggests self-respect, and by extension, indicates that you're a woman who understands her worth.

The moment a man realizes that he's with a woman who has clear boundaries, it becomes a quest to become the kind of man worthy of her.

He not only chases you, but he also starts to see you as someone he would be fortunate to secure a future with.

So, if he's treating you less than you deserve, communicate your boundaries clearly.

You're not just any woman; you're a high-value woman.

And a high-value woman requires a high-value approach.

4. HAVE STANDARDS: THE MAP TO HIS SUCCESS

You may think having standards is a given, but you'd be surprised at how many women lose sight of them when they're dating.

Having standards is about knowing what you will and won't tolerate — and being crystal clear about it.

Why it works: Men often liken dating to a challenge or a game — not in a manipulative or trivial way, but as a quest for success.

When you clearly communicate your standards, you give him a set of guidelines, a roadmap to success.

Men appreciate this clarity and view it as a scaffold for building a relationship.

In a way, you're doing him a favor: you're telling him exactly how to win you over, and that's incredibly empowering for him.

5. BELIEVING THAT YOU DESERVE IT: THE ULTIMATE ATTRACTOR

We often get what we think we deserve, for better or worse. If you believe you're worthy of love, respect, and kindness, that's what you'll attract.

Why it works: Believing you deserve the best makes you infinitely more attractive. It exudes a quiet confidence that speaks before you do.

When you radiate this type of self-assurance, it creates an aura around you that's irresistibly attractive.

Men will feel that they need to rise to the occasion to meet your standards. Your belief in yourself and your worth sends a clear message: you won't settle for anything less than you deserve, making you a rare and valuable find in the dating world.

In essence, having this internal conviction shapes not just your dating experience, but the man's as well.

He's not just chasing you; he's chasing the idea of a fulfilling, balanced relationship that's built on mutual respect and admiration.

Armed with these five qualities, you'll not only make him chase you but also become the catch he never even knew he was missing.

And the best part?

You'll be a better, more self-assured version of yourself, ready for a love that matches your high standards.

"I thank Matthew so much. His program changed my life.
His advice and techniques are invaluable.
Easy to understand and implement."

- Kim

Say THIS to Him to Make Him Want to Chase You

"You teach people how to treat you by what you allow, what you stop, and what you reinforce."

- Tony Gaskins

Words have power, especially in the dating arena. While body language and physical attraction often speak volumes, the right words can tip the scales in your favor.

If you're aiming for a relationship where your man is chasing you (not out of obligation, but because he genuinely wants to), the words you use can be your best asset.

1. EXPRESS A PREFERENCE: TEACH HIM HOW TO WIN YOUR HEART

There's a subtle yet impactful difference between setting boundaries and expressing preferences.

While boundaries are non-negotiable, preferences guide the way, and make it more likely he'll meet your standards without feeling like he's checking off a to-do list.

Examples:

"I only date guys who act like a gentleman."

This statement is gold, particularly during the initial stages of dating. It not only communicates what you're looking for but also lets him know what he can do to win your heart. Plus, it reaffirms that treating you well isn't optional—it's a necessity.

"I don't like guys who are just looking for a hookup."

The art of dropping this statement is timing. Say it when the conversation naturally leans that way, and watch how he reacts. His response will give you insights into whether he's aligned with your preferences or not.

Show, Don't Just Tell: Your Reactions Speak Louder

Sometimes, it's not about what you say but how you react. If he suggests a date venue or activity that's not your cup of tea, don't just decline—explain why. This teaches him about your likes and dislikes, giving him a roadmap to your heart.

Example:

"I wouldn't do that. I prefer..."

Let's say he suggests an outdoor date, but you're not an outdoorsy person. Instead of a flat 'no,' say something like, "I'm not much for the great outdoors, but I love art galleries."

You haven't just rejected him; you've given him an alternative, a way to succeed with you.

Remember, the goal here isn't to create a laundry list of demands, but to articulate your standards and preferences in a way that resonates with him.

Men appreciate clarity and direction, especially when it comes to navigating the maze of modern dating.

These statements are more than words; they're signals, helping him understand how to become the man you're looking for.

And when he gets it right?

That's when he'll feel like he's truly earned a place in your life, making him all the more eager to chase after you.

2. ENFORCE YOUR BOUNDARY: SET THE RULES, MAINTAIN THE GAME

Boundaries aren't barriers; they're signposts on the journey towards a healthy relationship. By clearly defining and enforcing your boundaries, you signal to a man that you value yourself highly and aren't willing to settle for less.

This doesn't mean he'll view you as a challenge to conquer, but rather as a partner worth respecting.

Scenario: The Midnight Booty Call

Say What You Want: "That sounds like a lot of fun and I'd love to come over some night in the future, but..."

State the Boundary: "…I'd rather we meet up during the day for now…"

Give a Reason: "…so we can get to know each other a little better first."

Propose an Alternative: "How about we meet up during the day this weekend?"

By doing this, you establish an agreement he must respect.

Will it deter some men?

Certainly. But those men were never going to give you the relationship you desire.

The ones who stick around? They're the keepers.

3. QUALIFY HIM: LIGHT-HEARTED INTERROGATION FOR HEAVY-DUTY RESULTS

Asking screening questions doesn't mean conducting a job interview. These questions should feel playful yet purposeful, revealing his suitability for a long-term commitment.

Questions to Consider:

"So, tell me. Are you a good boyfriend?"

This question sets the tone for a more serious relationship. If he jokes about being a bad boyfriend, take it as a red flag.

"Are you a gentleman?"

A follow-up to your expressed preference for gentlemen. Reinforce his positive answers, and mildly disapprove of negative ones.

"Are you the jealous type?"

Jealousy reveals a lot about a person's insecurities. His answer will tell you how he views relationships.

"What's the nicest thing you've ever done for a woman?"

This is a challenging question that lets you gauge his attitude toward previous relationships.

"What's your first impression of me?"

This invites flattery, flirtation, and a glimpse into how he perceives you.

"How do you know if you like someone?"

His answer here gives you a clue about his 'tells' for attraction, so you know what to look for in your future interactions.

Remember, your questions and boundaries aren't a test he must pass; they're guidelines to ensure you both want the same things from this relationship.

Qualifying and screening may sound like you're window-shopping for a partner, but in truth, it's more like you're laying the foundation for a partnership built to last.

4. MAINTAIN YOUR STANDARDS: THE INVISIBLE LADDER TO LOVE

Setting standards is an act of self-respect, but it only works if you remain steadfast in maintaining them.

The moment you waver or make exceptions, you send a mixed message, not just to him, but to yourself.

Consistency in upholding your standards creates a challenge that men will respect and strive to meet.

Pro Tip: Keep an active and fulfilled life outside of dating. Your happiness should never hinge on a relationship.

This makes your time more valuable and gives you the space to establish and uphold your standards effortlessly.

5. THE SACRED SELF: THE FOUNTAINHEAD OF TRUE LOVE

You are not a pit-stop on someone's journey, but a destination.

Elevating your sense of self to something sacred isn't vanity, it's self-awareness.

When you regard your time, attention, and emotions as invaluable, you teach people how to treat you.

Elements of the Sacred Self:

1. Who You Are is Sacred: You're not a convenience or an option; you're a priority.

2. Your Time is Sacred: Never allow someone to waste it. Time is an unrecoverable asset.

3. Your Attention is Sacred: It's your emotional currency. Spend it where it earns interest.

4. Your Emotions are Sacred: Your feelings are valid, important, and deserve respect.

5. You Deserve Excellence: Only allow people into your life who lift you higher and positively influence your well-being.

Manifestation Through Belief: When you truly, deeply believe that you are sacred, you project that belief onto the world.

This isn't about self-centeredness; it's about self-assuredness. You radiate a quiet confidence that beckons men to rise to the occasion, to treat you with the respect and love you not only seek but fundamentally deserve.

In the world of dating, you're not merely navigating a landscape; you're also cultivating your own garden.

By maintaining your standards and believing in your sacred self, you're telling the world—and the man who deserves to be in your life—that you are a stunning garden that deserves the highest care.

Men will either rise to cultivate it or reveal themselves as unworthy gardeners.

Either way, you win.

"I love how much I learned about how men think and what they are truly looking for. I have been in management for 27 years. A male dominant environment. By focusing on your principles, I have finally had some great first, second and even third dates. It is still not natural for me, but it is getting easier to transition from work to woman."

- Deanna

4 Powerful Steps to Make a Man Chase You

"Love is an endless mystery, for it has nothing else to explain it."

– Rabindranath Tagore

Getting a man to not just chase you but also invest in you for the long term requires an intricate balance of giving and taking, of sharing and retaining, a dance of mutual respect and attraction.

Below is a four-step formula designed to get him to chase you while laying the foundation for a committed, lasting relationship.

1. SHOW INTEREST WITHOUT STRINGS ATTACHED

Why Men Love It: Men are often as self-conscious and eager to be liked as women are. A genuine compliment or a sign of interest can be the nudge he needs to make his move.

The Balanced Approach: Being interested doesn't mean being desperate.

It's crucial to differentiate between the two. Interest is free from expectations; it's an invitation, not a demand.

If he doesn't respond the way you'd hoped, it's disappointing, but not devastating.

Practical Tips:
- A warm smile when you see him
- Touching his arm during a conversation
- Making eye contact and holding it for a second longer than usual

The Catch: Showing interest is not a guarantee for reciprocation. Your intention is to send a signal, not force an outcome. If he's interested, he'll step up to the plate. If not, that's useful information too.

By taking this approach, you're setting the stage for him to chase you because he knows there's something worth pursuing. It's like leaving the door ajar; he still has to walk through it.

You're essentially stating: "Here's an opportunity. What you do with it is up to you."

The power lies in both your hands, creating a balanced dynamic that can lead to a loving, committed relationship.

2. GIVE HIM OPPORTUNITIES TO CHASE AND PURSUE YOU

Why Men Love It: The chase is deeply ingrained in the male psyche, it's part of their evolutionary fabric. When men are given tasks or challenges, it taps into their natural instinct to pursue and to win.

The Balanced Approach: While you're giving him opportunities to chase, it shouldn't feel like a never-ending series of hoops to jump through. The tasks or invitations should be genuine needs or desires you have, presented in a way that makes him feel like he's winning something valuable: your appreciation and deeper interest.

Practical Tips:

The Direct Invitation: "I'm at this fantastic café right now. You should come and check it out with me." By doing this, you not only show your interest but also allow him to step up and come to you.

The Help Request: "Could you help me with something?" This taps into his desire to be needed and useful.

If you're just getting to know him, keep it simple. As you grow closer, more significant tasks can become part of the equation, which can solidify his investment in the relationship.

The Suggestive Mention: Drop hints about activities you'd like to do or places you'd like to go. For example, "I've always wanted to go to a jazz club but never really got the chance." This will give him the opportunity to plan something special for you.

The Catch: Make sure these opportunities to chase aren't tests or games, but authentic invitations for him to step up and be a part of your life. Men can usually tell when they're being manipulated, and that could be counterproductive to creating a genuine connection.

The strategy here is not about playing hard to get but about providing a series of meaningful interactions that allow him to prove his worth, and for you to gauge his level of interest and commitment.

It sets up a chase scenario that's exhilarating but also deeply rooted in respect and mutual interest.

3. ALLOW HIM TO MAKE PROGRESS AND REAP THE REWARDS

Why Men Love It: When a man feels he's making strides in winning your heart, it boosts his confidence and commitment to the journey. Men are goal-oriented; they relish the sense of achievement and value the prize all the more if they've had to work for it.

The Balanced Approach: Your rewards and emotional displays should not be tools to manipulate him but genuine reactions to his positive actions. This creates a cycle of goodwill and meaningful effort from both sides.

Practical Tips:

Timely Rewards: When he does something noteworthy, reward him with your appreciation. It could be verbal praise, a heartfelt thank-you, or even something as simple as a radiant smile. These rewards should escalate naturally with the deepening of the relationship.

Emotional Openness: Don't be afraid to show your emotions, but do so without expectations or strings attached. Your emotions are not bargaining chips; they're your genuine reactions to the world and him. This invites him to connect on a more profound emotional level and lets him know it's okay for him to do the same.

Specific Compliments: "That's really considerate of you," or, "You look incredibly handsome tonight," are ways to express your interest and to reinforce behaviors or qualities that you find attractive in him. The more specific you are, the clearer your message, and the more likely he is to repeat those positive actions.

The Catch: While it's crucial for him to make progress, it's equally important for you to maintain your standards and boundaries. His progress should not come at the cost of your well-being or self-respect.

Your encouragement and emotional expression create a powerful mix that not only maintains his interest but also deepens it. It adds a layer of complexity and depth to the relationship that moves it beyond the superficial.

By allowing him to make progress in a way that is aligned with your own needs and standards, you both win. The relationship evolves into something meaningful, based on mutual respect, effort, and emotional investment.

4. BE ATTAINABLE WITHOUT COMPROMISING YOUR WORTH

Why Men Love It: Men appreciate a challenge, but they also need to see a light at the end of the tunnel. If a man senses that you're out of reach or aren't willing to let him into your world, he may lose hope and pull back. By being attainable, you offer him the vision of a fulfilling relationship that feels both challenging and achievable.

The Balanced Approach: It's crucial to walk the line between being attainable and not selling yourself short. You should never compromise on your core values and standards just to appear more attainable.

Practical Tips:

Progressive Warmth: It's fine to enjoy playful banter and teasing, especially in the early stages of dating.

However, as the relationship deepens, it's essential to shift gears. Gradually display a softer, warmer side of yourself as he invests emotionally and practically in the relationship.

Emotional Depth: Gradually share your vulnerabilities and fears. Open up about your dreams, your past, and your thoughts on a future together.

This forms a deeper emotional bond and offers him a glimpse of what life with you would entail.

Pacing: If he's putting in the effort and showing enthusiasm, reciprocate with similar energy. However, if he seems to be pulling away, give him the space he needs.

Mimic his pace without playing games, but remember, this is not about punishing him for pulling away or overly rewarding him for coming closer; it's about respecting both your needs at the moment.

The Catch: Being attainable should not be mistaken for being easy.

The more he invests in the relationship, the more you should be willing to reciprocate, but always in a manner that respects your own integrity and well-being.

By blending these four ingredients—showing genuine interest, offering ways for him to chase you, allowing room for progress, and being attainably intriguing—you create a potent formula for meaningful emotional investment.

This doesn't guarantee that every man will chase you, but it does ensure that the man who does is genuinely interested, invested, and envisioning a future together.

The balance is in finding the right measure of each element, customized to the specific dynamics between you and him.

By doing so, you pave the way for a relationship that's not just exciting, but also deeply fulfilling for both of you.

"I have paid for other online love courses and it was either playing tricks, art of manipulation with hypnotic words and this just feels more realistic, more simple and more easier to understand. Nothing really should be too complicated. This program has helped me open my eyes to the few mistakes I have made."

- Kelli

Success Stories From Not Chasing

Let's talk about how this has actually worked using stories from other women…

THE MELODY OF TWO HEARTS

Sophia had always been a lover of the arts, but her real passion lay in painting. She was equally captivated by music, which is how she first encountered Leo, a musician whose hands danced on the piano keys like a painter's brush on canvas.

Leo had a way of connecting with his audience, making each note seem like an intimate secret. However, when it came to emotional intimacy off-stage, Leo was as elusive as a fading echo.

For months, Sophia attended Leo's gigs at various venues—jazz bars, intimate concerts, even outdoor festivals. They had exchanged numbers, enjoyed coffees together, and talked endlessly about the beauty of art.

Yet, Leo was like a beautiful song with a complicated arrangement; thrilling but emotionally unattainable. Their meetings were always on his terms, often squeezed in between his recording sessions and interviews. She felt like a supporting act in his grand musical journey, forever waiting for a duet that would never happen.

Sophia finally recognized the dissonance. For someone who spent her life appreciating the harmony in art, she couldn't ignore the lack of it in her emotional life.

She made a hard but necessary decision—to stop chasing Leo and redirect her energies towards her own artistic endeavors. Her canvas, once filled with hues influenced by her infatuation with him, now reverted to colors that defined her.

After months of dedicated work, Sophia got an opportunity to showcase her art in a local gallery. She filled the room with paintings that resonated with her soul; her art was a colorful blend of emotion and technique, exactly like the woman herself.

At the gallery opening, as Sophia explained the inspiration behind her favorite piece—a riotous blend of reds and golds representing resilience—she noticed Ethan, a visitor who seemed genuinely enchanted by her art.

Ethan was different. He was an architect with a deep appreciation for all forms of design and structure—be it a building or a beautiful painting.

Their conversation naturally flowed from art to life, music to architecture, and everything in between. It was like a duet where both partners knew exactly when to lead and when to follow.

Ethan was emotionally present in a way Leo never was. He would call her to ask about her day, listen intently as she shared her creative ideas, and even offered to help set up her next art exhibition.

With Ethan, Sophia felt an emotional synergy; there was room for both to flourish, a shared stage where neither had to dim their lights for the other to shine.

As months passed, Sophia realized that true love should feel like a seamless duet, where both voices enrich the melody.

With Ethan, she found a partner who not only applauded her solo performances but also eagerly joined her in harmonious duets, in art and in life.

Sophia finally understood the value of emotional availability. She realized that while it's essential to be captivated by someone, it's even more vital to be emotionally in tune with them.

In Ethan, she found her co-musician, her co-artist, and her co-navigator in the journey of love, teaching her the ultimate lesson—love is the most beautiful art form, and it requires two equally committed artists.

THE RECIPE FOR CERTAINTY

Anna had always been a go-getter, a woman whose professional life was the epitome of precision and planning. Her counterpart was Alex, a senior executive at a tech startup, who matched her wit for wit, ambition for ambition.

At least, that's what it looked like on paper and during business mixers where they initially crossed paths. Alex had everything going for him—a successful career, good looks, and a seemingly endless list of accomplishments. But when it came to matters of the heart, he was as indecisive as a leaf in the wind.

For months, Anna found herself caught in Alex's cycle of hot and cold. One week, he would talk about future plans, whisking her away to art exhibitions and fancy dinners as if they were building something together.

The next week, he would pull away, drowning her in an unsettling silence, citing work pressures or personal issues as reasons for his emotional distance.

Anna spent nights wondering if she should continue investing her emotions in a 'maybe,' in a future that flickered like a faulty light bulb.

Eventually, Anna decided she had had enough. The woman who wouldn't accept a maybe in her boardroom meetings wouldn't accept one in her personal life either.

She made a conscious decision to stop pursuing Alex and invest time in herself. Anna had always been interested in culinary arts but never found the time to explore it.

A local culinary institute was offering gourmet cooking classes, and she enrolled, excited to diversify her already impressive skill set.

It was there that Anna met Ben, a literature professor with a love for cooking and a personality as warm as the dishes he prepared.

Right from their first interaction, Ben showed a level of emotional availability and straightforwardness that Anna found refreshing.

When they were assigned as partners for a class project that involved cooking a complex French meal, the chemistry was undeniable— not just in their culinary creations, but in the ease with which they communicated and collaborated.

Ben was different; he didn't dwell in the realm of 'maybe.' After a few cooking sessions and deeper conversations, Ben expressed his intentions clearly.

He was interested in Anna, not just as a cooking partner, but as someone he saw a future with. "I know what I want, Anna," he said one evening after class, "I want to share a lifetime of meals and endless conversations with you."

His words felt like the missing ingredient in Anna's recipe for love. It dawned on her that a fulfilling relationship doesn't live in the land of uncertainty; it thrives in the commitment of a clear 'yes.'

As time passed, Anna found in Ben a partner who matched her emotional and intellectual appetite. They didn't just cook together; they built a life seasoned with love, respect, and unmistakable certainty.

Anna had discovered her own recipe for happiness: a relationship built on the solid foundation of clear intentions and mutual emotional investment.

And as she stood beside Ben, years later, cooking in their own kitchen, she realized that the most satisfying dish is one prepared with love and certainty.

DEFENDING WORTH, FINDING VALUE

Jade was a modern woman with traditional values—intelligent, well-read, and passionate about social issues. Her life had its fair share of excitement, but nothing matched the adrenaline rush she felt around Ryan, a tattooed musician with a rebellious streak.

Ryan was a whirlwind of unpredictability, making Jade feel alive in a way no one else had. However, this thrill came at a cost. Ryan's behavior was inconsistent, and his tendency to push boundaries often left Jade feeling disrespected and devalued.

She endured the casual demeaning comments, the sporadic communication, and even his tendency to take her for granted, rationalizing it as part of his "bad-boy" persona.

After all, love was supposed to be a challenge, right? At least that's what she tried to convince herself, while the pattern of disrespect slowly chipped away at her self-esteem.

One evening, after another cancelled plan and a dismissive text message from Ryan, Jade found herself staring at her reflection.

The strong, confident woman she had always identified with seemed to have faded. That's when she made a conscious choice—she decided to stop chasing a relationship that was slowly draining her spirit.

Jade had always been intrigued by martial arts and its philosophy of self-discipline and respect.

Driven by an urge to reclaim her self-worth, she enrolled in a self-defense class. The dojo, as it turned out, would not only be a place where she learned to defend herself physically but emotionally as well.

In her class was Mark, a corporate lawyer by profession but a martial artist at heart. From the moment they met, Mark's demeanor was the antithesis of Ryan's. He was a gentleman, respectful both in and out of the dojo.

Their partnership in the class quickly turned into a friendship and then blossomed into something more meaningful. Mark admired Jade for her intelligence, her kindness, and the strength that she emanated, both as a martial artist and as a woman.

"What I love about martial arts," Mark said to her one evening after class, "is that it teaches you respect—for your opponent, for the art, and most importantly, for yourself."

Those words struck a chord deep within her. With Mark, Jade never had to question her worth or defend her place in his life.

NEVER CHASE A MAN

Their relationship was a mutual celebration of respect and love, worlds apart from the emotional battleground she had left behind.

As they grew closer, Mark became not just her partner, but also her greatest supporter, uplifting her in every aspect of life.

Their relationship was a constant reminder that real love never asks you to compromise your self-respect. It only amplifies your worth.

Years later, as Jade stood beside Mark, both dressed in martial arts gis and exchanging vows in a unique wedding ceremony, she knew she had found her equal.

She was grateful for the journey that led her to a love that truly valued her, in every sense of the word.

FROM GAMES TO GENUINE

Maria, a social worker dedicated to creating impact, had always been the kind of woman who loved deeply and genuinely. Her enthusiasm for life was infectious, and that's what initially caught Steve's attention.

Steve was charming, mysterious, and just enigmatic enough to keep Maria on her toes. At first, the chase was exhilarating. It felt like a complex game, each move calculated, every text a clue to decipher.

As time went on, Maria realized that while she was planning a future, Steve was more invested in maintaining the mystery.

His ambiguous statements and elusive behaviors were part of a bigger game he relished. It seemed as though Steve enjoyed the chase more than he enjoyed the possibility of a meaningful relationship.

Each time Maria felt they were making progress, Steve would withdraw or change the rules. She began to feel like a pawn rather than a partner.

One evening, after yet another confusing conversation with Steve, Maria had an epiphany. She was investing her energy into a relationship that felt more like a game of chess than a genuine human connection.

Feeling emotionally drained, Maria decided to disengage from this perplexing emotional maze. She realized she deserved someone whose love was straightforward, not a puzzle to be solved.

Around this time, Maria had been actively involved in a charity organization aimed at empowering underprivileged youth.

Her work had always been her sanctuary, a place where she found purpose and fulfillment. It was at one of the charity events that she crossed paths with David, a pediatrician who volunteered his time providing free check-ups for the kids.

David was different; there were no games, no smoke and mirrors. What Maria saw was what she got—a man with a passion for service, just like her.

As they collaborated on more projects, their admiration for each other grew, founded on the authentic selves they both brought to the table.

David would often say, "When you're working toward something bigger than yourself, you find the right people to make the journey worthwhile."

His words resonated deeply with Maria. She felt seen, understood, and valued—not as a piece in a game, but as an equal collaborator in this journey called life.

As their relationship blossomed, so did their collaborative projects. Together they launched initiatives that combined Maria's social work expertise and David's medical skills. Their relationship was a synergy of not just love, but also of vision and values.

The love Maria and David shared wasn't about keeping score; it was about lifting each other up and building something that could make the world a better place.

And in finding that, Maria discovered that real love is not a game; it's a meaningful collaboration that enriches both partners and everyone around them.

THE TRUTH ABOUT NOT CHASING

The notion of not chasing might seem counterintuitive in a culture that often glorifies the "hunt" as part of the romance. However, these stories underscore a fundamental truth—sometimes the best way to find what you're truly looking for is to stop chasing it.

It's important to understand that not chasing doesn't mean giving up on love or lowering your standards.

Quite the opposite—it means elevating your sense of self-worth and valuing your time, energy, and emotional investment.

When you stop chasing, you allow room for what is genuinely meant for you to come into your life. In doing so, you make space for connections that are grounded in mutual respect, shared values, and emotional availability.

The reality is, not chasing might mean you won't end up with the guy you initially had your eyes on. And that's okay.

Because when you honor yourself, life often rewards you with something—or someone—far better than you could have imagined.

Each man you meet is a lesson, a signpost pointing you either toward what you genuinely desire or back to the patterns you're meant to outgrow.

These are life's subtle tests: Will you choose familiarity over your own well-being, or will you courageously step into the unknown where something far more enriching awaits?

The act of not chasing is an act of self-love. It's a choice to invest in your personal growth, to spend time on activities and people that enrich you, and to allow a relationship to be a part of your life, not the centerpiece that defines your worth.

By doing so, you become the chooser, not the chaser. You create an emotional environment where mutual love, respect, and fulfilling partnerships can flourish.

Remember, love should feel like a harmonious duet, not a solo performance where you're the only one singing your heart out.

Your ideal relationship won't require you to chase incessantly; it will simply ask that you be yourself, valuing you for who you are and not what you can provide.

If you find yourself in a situation where you're tempted to chase, take a step back and consider what you're really pursuing.

Is it love, or is it the validation that comes from the chase itself? When you let go of the need to chase, you open up a world of possibilities— possibilities where you can be loved and valued just as you are.

The next time life tests you, choose yourself. You might just find that when you stop chasing, what you've been searching for has the space to find you.

"Hey Matt, I did everything you said and he came, professed his love, and paid my bills. We're on the same page now and it is exhilarating."

- Dee Dee

Moving Forward

You've navigated through the fascinating landscape of modern dating, equipped with proven strategies and transformative insights tailored for women who want more than just a date—they seek a meaningful, enduring relationship.

This book isn't just your compass; it's your specialized GPS in the complex journey that is contemporary love.

Remember, each new date is more than just an encounter; it's an untouched horizon, a potential tapestry of shared moments and emotional connection.

Your arsenal includes emotional intelligence, unwavering authenticity, and an earnest wish to cultivate a deep connection with someone special.

As you step out into the world of dating with your newfound wisdom, understand that the ultimate triumph is not just in finding a compatible partner but also in discovering and honoring your own needs, aspirations, and value.

This is a masterclass not just in becoming an irresistible date but also in evolving into a magnificent long-term partner.

The true alchemy occurs when two souls don't just meet, but profoundly resonate with each other's essence. If you've reached this point in the book, it's a testament to your commitment to elevating your romantic life and cultivating a relationship filled with depth and purpose. That dedication is already more than half the battle.

Embrace the principles contained within these pages, and your romantic horizon won't merely be filled with hope; it will brim with genuine promise.

Take the courageous step, unleash your incredible self, and let love follow its natural course.

Your path to a resilient, rewarding relationship isn't just a fanciful dream; with the insights and strategies in this guide, it becomes a compelling likelihood.

When it comes to love, I'm all about helping you stack all of the odds in your favor so that you WILL end up in the relationship you've always wanted.

So here's to the meaningful connections and incredible love stories yet to be written—yours included.

May your journey in love not only be enchanting but enduring, a testament to the magical potential when two lives genuinely converge.

If you enjoyed this book, I'd appreciate it if you would go back to Amazon and give me a good review…

https://www.amazon.com/Never-Chase-Man-Attracting-Cherishes/dp/B08ZW84NK8/

WANT MORE GUIDANCE?

If you're looking for some more help, guidance, and mentorship on your journey to attracting the man you want and getting into the relationship that fulfills you, make sure to visit my main website and join my email newsletter...

https://commitmentconnection.com/

Here's a list of books that you can purchase from me on Amazon...

https://www.amazon.com/stores/Matthew-Coast/author/B00C18S790

Here's our Facebook community...

https://www.facebook.com/groups/goddesscommunity

Here's a list of audio, video, and text based programs if you're interested in diving deeper into that...

https://commitmentconnection.com/matthew-coasts-programs/

And if you'd like us to guide you through the process of attracting a great partner through coaching, visit...

https://matthewcoast.com/

Talk soon,

Matthew Coast

Made in the USA
Middletown, DE
01 October 2024

61804917R00056